Plugging In...

Connecting To Your
Universal Gifts

JEANNE PROVOST

In Gratitude:

To my parents and siblings, thank you for all the beautiful lessons I've gathered and grown from. I love you all.

To my children Sally and Christina, my son in law, Rhett, and Grandbaby Ruby...I love you to the moon and back forever and always!

To the love of my life, Brian, thank you for all your encouragement, kindness, your laughter, friendship and love. I am so grateful we get to share our life together!

Thank you to my editors, Danielle and Paulina; you are both wonderful, and I appreciate all your patience and hard work!

*Note to readers:

I love God

I love Jesus

I love Mary

I love the Holy Spirit

I love Christianity and all religions

I love the Universe

I love Buddha

I love Quan Yin, the Goddess of Mercy, Compassion and Kindness

I love the Tao

I love Shamanism

I love Prayer

I love Meditation

I love Journaling

I believe God is part of all good.

TABLE OF CONTENTS

INTRODUCTION:

Why Is It Important to Be Aware and Understand our Universal Gifts?

When I was five, my mother read *The Secret Garden* to my siblings and me. She sat in the hallway between the girls' and boys' bedrooms, her clear voice carrying the story of the poor, orphaned girl and the crippled, depressed boy to our eager ears. This is my earliest memory of being touched by the power and beauty of what I came to know later in life as our "Universal Gifts."

Although mom read us many books, this book in particular stayed with me my whole life. In the story Mary is an orphan and her cousin Colin has been bedridden for years, hidden away by his fearful father. As Mom read each night, the rise and fall of her voice created colorful images in my mind and I felt deeply connected to these two children. I felt the full range of Mary and Colin's emotions from pain to hope while watching an unkempt, valueless and wild ramble of weeds became a glorious garden filled with bright colors and bountiful fruit. As these two children meet in an old forgotten garden and trim back the branches, the garden comes alive and bursts into beautiful grandeur. Simultaneously, the same thing happens to the children: Colin begins to walk and Mary finds joy and happiness.

This book demonstrates how each of us has the ability – no matter what our circumstances – to step out of worry and self-pity and into a more beautiful life. As I've grown older, I learned that by conjuring up loving thoughts, by being positive and weeding out negative emotions, and fertilizing myself daily through prayer, meditation and journaling... by watering, feeding and tending to my own "garden" daily, I could create a beautiful life for myself and everyone I touch in this lifetime.

There comes a point in a person's life – whether it's brought about by a traumatic injury, a significant life change or just plain boredom – when you begin to hunger for something more. You don't feel satisfied but trapped in the life you've created. If you've ever had inkling or feeling that you want more out of this life, or perhaps you look around feeling envious of others moving through challenges and tragedies with ease and grace, like it effortless for them, remember that they were once in the same spot as you, the only difference is they have taken the time to connect to these gifts and use them daily in their lives. As you read each chapter of this book and begin to connect deeper within, do your best to let go of judgments of others, and concentrate on your own personal life and what you want to create. Soon you will begin allowing these Divine gifts to seep in to your perceptions, to your most chronic thoughts and feelings, and out into your life. As you do this, you too will be simultaneously weeding out what no longer serves you and fertilizing your desires to create a beautiful life.

Once you have this knowledge at your disposal, anytime you are feeling low or discouraged you will have the tools to go deeper and reflect, emerging in a higher and brighter light than ever before. And if you have already tasted new growth or movement in your life and it feels good to you, then this book will guide you even further and more swiftly on your journey. Like a pebble hitting a still pond, the changes you make within yourself will ripple out to everyone around you, and in a very real way, you will be part of making this world a more beautiful place.

What follows is a practical exploration of the "laws" that govern the process of all creation and are evident in every part of this glorious universe. These are gifts in the purest sense of the word: they are here, free for the taking, for each and every one of us. No one is left out, but it is up to us to "plug-in" and put our energy into creating the life we truly want to experience here on earth.

CHAPTER 1:

The Law of Attraction

The first Universal Gift is the law of attraction. Many of you reading this have heard these words, studied these words, and seen them work at times in your life. When I first came across the words the "law of attraction," I thought they sounded pretty "out there" and New Age, and I did not relate to them. But when I read about this law in the wildly popular book The Secret, and watched the interviews of the transformational experts featured in the movie, I connected deeply with the essence of this universal principle. The law of attraction was the basis of how I had always lived my life – although mostly unconsciously. As I studied this principle in greater depth, I came to understand that the law of attraction could easily be summed up in a couple of key phrases:

- "Where your attention goes, energy flows."
- "That which is like unto itself is drawn."

Even in our everyday language, we use many common expressions that speak directly to the Law of Attraction. "Like

1

attracts like," for example, or "Birds of a feather flock together." But what we may not understand is that what makes people similar – and therefore attracted to each other – is not as superficial as the clothes we wear or the professions we choose. We are drawn to some experiences and repulsed by others at a much more fundamental level of our being. In fact, it is the most fundamental level of all: the level of vibration.

Everything that exists in this seemingly physical and material Universe, when studied at its most basic subatomic structure, is made up of energy, and all energy vibrates at a particular frequency. Everything that you can see, hear, taste, touch, and smell is made up of energy – the desk you are sitting at, for example, and the computer screen you're looking at. And all of it is moving at a particular frequency, which your senses translate into experience. But even more important than understanding the energy frequency of inanimate objects around us is that we understand the energy frequency that we are *emitting* in every moment of every day by virtue of the thoughts we think, the mood and attitude we carry, and the emotions we feel.

Good-feeling emotions, such as joy, exhilaration, excitement, and anticipation, are nothing more than energy in motion (e+motion) that moves at a higher rate of frequency. And conversely, emotions that we would describe as bad feeling, such as anger, sadness, fear, or depression, are nothing but energy that is moving or vibrating at a slower, lower rate of speed.

The law of attraction states that whatever energy we broadcast out into the Universe is joined by and becomes attractive to energies that are harmonic or resonant in frequency – i.e., birds of a feather flock together! Slow moving energy attracts more of the same, and so does high-flying energy. This is why we sometimes have the experience of having "one of those days" where nothing we do seems to feel good or work out well. This is simply the law of attraction in action: the more we give our attention to what isn't working, the worse we feel, and the more not-working things are drawn to us. The whole reason I came to learning about these gifts was through a deep, downward spiral, which is why I now have inner peace even when external conflicts arise in my life. There are always gifts in the hard times we go through – if we are open to receiving them.

Luckily, this law works just as well at creating upward-spirals, which is why you sometimes feel like you are "on a roll" or "in the zone." Your mood is good; your thoughts are positive; your expectations are high; and as a result, you magnetize people, circumstances and experiences that reflect back to you, to your good-feeling inner state of being.

My spiritual background includes growing up Catholic, and attending Catholic grade school, where my parents dropped us off early in the morning each day so we could kneel and pray at daily mass before school started. In junior high and high school I never missed my weekly CCD classes and went to Sunday Mass. This is when I began writing to God every time I was having a hard time. I never wanted anyone to see or read what I was feeling so I would tear it out of my notebook and burn it in our fireplace downstairs. I was a senior when I started having dreams with messages that were very powerful, and felt a deep connection to the spirit world. I had not heard of intuition yet, but later I realized I was recognizing my inner GPS, and following what was being asked of me. When I had children of my own, I taught Sunday school, 7th and 8th grade Religious Ed and, later, Confirmation. I loved the Catholic faith and it was all I knew.

When I was in college, my Grandfather taught me a prayer that I've always called my "morning prayer" and which I still recite as I greet each day:

"Good morning, Dear Jesus. This day is for you.

I want you to bless all that I think, say, and do.

Come Holy Spirit, creator-blessed,

And in my heart take up thy rest."

In this prayer I was again introduced to the idea that our thoughts become our words, and later they become our actions.

You might be beginning to get a sense of just how important your thoughts, moods, and emotions really are. This is the "ah-ha!" moment of realization that flooded through me when I connected the dots between what I had learned when my mother read me *The Secret Garden*, to what my Granddad's prayer had taught me later. There is nothing more important than learning to deliberately offer your thoughts, moods, and emotions, for these are what set the tone for everything you create in your experience. The quality of your mood determines the quality of your life, in the same way that a dial on a radio determines whether your radio plays easy listening or rock. There are all sorts of stations on the radio to choose from, and you are making a choice each second about how you want to feel.

So, what does this mean? Simple. If you think thoughts of abundance – if you appreciate the abundance of air around you; the abundance of food or friends or sunshine – you are broadcasting the vibration of abundance to the far corners of the Universe, and the Universe will deliver back to you more experiences that look and feel abundant in nature. And the same principle holds true when you dwell in thoughts of lack or limitation. If you're angry or discouraged that something in your life is lacking or is not good enough in some way, anger and discouragement are the vibrations you are broadcasting into the Universe. And in response, the law of attraction will provide you an abundance of things that you feel are lacking and discouraging.

There is no end to the variety of experiences that the law of attraction can line up on our behalf. It delivers both what is wanted and what is unwanted, depending on what signal we are sending out. Simply put, if you want more freedom and joy in your life, you must learn to conjure the feelings of freedom and joy. In every single moment, there is something in your life that you can use as your excuse to conjure the feeling of freedom. Most of us have been conditioned to view the world through a lens of lack, but we have the power to shift this lens at every moment. It's like working a muscle; the more you practice, the easier it gets! We all have the choice to think, feel, imagine, and conjure the experience of abundance.

Putting the Law of Attraction into Action:

In order for the law of attraction to work in your life, remember that what you focus your attention on, you will draw more of. You are blessed with the power of free will and choice, which means that at every moment, you have the power to decide what you will focus on. There is wanted and unwanted energy in virtually every person, place, and situation. If you choose to focus on what you don't like, you will attract more of what you don't like. If you choose to focus on what's right, what's working and what feels good, you will attract more good-working, good-feeling experiences. In each moment, pay attention to what you are focused on, and make the commitment to deliberately look for what you want to see. It is all around you; I promise!

CHAPTER 2:

The Law of Deliberate Creation

The second Universal Gift is the law of deliberate creation, and once you understand this law, the fun really begins! As we explored in the previous chapter, the law of attraction is always at work – in all things, all the time – behind the scenes. Similar to the law of gravity, the law of attraction has an effect on us whether we are consciously aware of it or not, whether we understand it or not. The force of gravity keeps us from floating off into space. Attraction is the force that determines what we magnetize into our life experience. You can think of the law of attraction like a boomerang; the vibrations you are sending out into the Universe in each moment by virtue of your thoughts, feelings, moods, and energy are returned back to you through the people, scenarios, events, and experiences that you attract into your life. The law of deliberate creation takes this understanding one step further, by making us aware that we have the power to offer our vibration *on purpose*, so that we can create our lives deliberately, rather than by default.

Begin to pay attention to the people you come into regular contact with and you will quickly discover that the vast majority of them are offering their vibration – and therefore creating their lives – entirely by default. For example, if they witness something pleasing, they are pleased, and their vibration raises. And likewise, if they witness something that seems unjust, they become angry or sad in response, and their vibration plummets.

Without a working understanding of the law of deliberate creation, we approach life passively. Whether we want to admit it to ourselves or not, we are more victims of circumstances than the powerful creators of them. We simply observe what *is*, and allow this "reality" to hijack our moods and determine our vibration. And we do this whether we like or dislike what is happening! The problem with this approach is that the law of attraction responds to our vibration by giving us more of the same, whether it is wanted or not. This explains why some people cannot seem to make the changes they desire in their lives; they are so busy reacting to what already *is*, and as a result, they rob themselves of their innate power to create something different.

For example, imagine that your current "reality" is that you don't have all the money you desire, and in fact are deep in debt. If you focus on the fact that you don't have enough money to pay your bills and allow this condition to dominate your thoughts and feelings – if you consciously or unconsciously offer a vibration consistent with fear, worry, or doubt – the law of attraction responds to your vibration of lack by bringing you more evidence of lack. This is a perfect case-in-point of how we unknowingly *mis*-create, when we live without an awareness of these Universal laws and how they work. When we deliberately start focusing on what we *do* want to experience in our lives and offer a vibration that is in harmony with that, we are applying the law of deliberate creation.

One of my favorite all-time stories about the power of the law of deliberate creation took place four months before my daughter Sally's wedding. Sally was just beginning to heal after suffering a serious brain injury that left her incapacitated for nearly six years and required fifteen separate surgeries. She came to me one day and told me she was concerned about the wedding, and specifically about the finances. I told her not to worry and assured her that it would work itself out. It was the week before New Year's – a perfect time to "intend" a new creation! After our visit, I led myself through a beautiful meditation, in which I pictured every aspect of Sally's wedding... how everything and everyone would look and feel and sound... I saw the peacefulness and joy on her and her finance's faces... and I saw enough money to cover every last detail, literally raining down into my vision from every corner of the Universe.

As I was journaling after my meditation, I asked God, the Universe, for $20,000.00 so that I could help in providing this beautiful experience for my daughter and her new husband. I didn't care where it came from, and I was open to receive it in any way, shape, or form. I was summoning the power of deliberate creation, and I made the commitment not to allow a single negative thought to seep into the sacred space I had created. Anytime I would start to feel the slightest pang of fear or worry, I sent them packing, affirming to myself my one hundred percent trust that the money would come – and in fact, was already on its way.

It was a few days later when I got a letter in the mail, along with a check for $14,000.00, from the mortgage company I had used when I first got my home loan four years earlier. Apparently, they had overcharged me and were now issuing me a refund. Two days later, I called the HOA in the community where I lived to find out the amount my monthly fees were being raised, and as I was taking with the representative, she said, "You know, there is a $4,000 credit on your account; it looks like you were double-paying for a while." She then asked me how I would like the credit returned to me, and I told her a check would be fine. The week wasn't up and I had already created $18,000.00.

At the end of the week I received a referral from a client who bought a $2,000.00 package. That same day in the mail was a notice from my bank, explaining they had credited me $200.00 from an overpayment made electronically to my insurance company. And then, like a wink from the Universe, I found a dime on the sidewalk!

In a period of less than one week, I manifested over $20,000.00 of money that had been there all along but I never knew existed. Elated, I called Sally, and the energy of her happiness poured through the phone lines. Instantly, all the stress vanished from the wedding planning. On the day of the event, everything went so smoothly, and Sally and Rhett were able to have the beautiful day that they so deserved!

Stories like these are not fantastical; they are well within reach. It is when we believe that we only create with action alone that accounts like mine seem miraculous. In truth, you are your own creator of your own reality – and out of seeming nothingness you can harness the power of conscious intent to create whatever you want. As we will continue to explore throughout this book, every tangible creation occurs first in the inner realm of our thoughts, imagination, intentions, emotions and beliefs. When these are in alignment with what we intend to create, they manifest as words, behaviors, and inspired actions that lead us inexplicably to all that we desire.

Putting the Law of Deliberate Creation into Action:

Here are five steps to applying this powerful law to create any outcome that you desire:

- First, become centered by meditating and journaling. Quieting your mind allows you to connect to your inner-most self – your soul self – that knows your deepest desires. In your journal, write out anything you want to let go of, feel the energy of these things leave your body, then begin writing your new intentions.
- Second, declare your intention. What is it that you want more (or less) of? As you consider this improved condition or expanded reality, allow yourself to feel

WHY you want this. What quality do you believe you would have more of if you created exactly what you want?

- Next, focus your mind on being grateful for having already received this. Your subconscious mind does not know the difference between an actual experience and an experience that you are clearly imagining. If you've ever seen a well-made horror movie, you already know this to be true! The more you interact with your creation-in-process as if it is already part of your experience, the faster you will draw it to you.

- When thoughts or feelings of doubt and fear creep in, discipline yourself to keep returning your focus to your intended creation, not the absence of it.

- Imagine what it would feel like if your desire was already created, picture it like a movie in front of you. When you receive what feels like an inspiration or strong urge to take an action in that direction, TAKE IT! This is your intuition speaking to you from your deepest self.

- Lastly, *trust the process. Believe* the law of deliberate creation is summoning resources from wherever they are right now in order to support the unfolding of your manifestation.

CHAPTER 3:

The Law of Allowing

The third Universal Gift that is important to understand is the Law of Allowing. This is the principle of least action, of no resistance, and it is essential to the creation of anything we desire. A lot of people are of the mindset that the most powerful law in the Universe is the law of attraction. This is the law that everyone was talking about after reading the book *The Secret,* and it's what most people thought *The Secret* was about. In fact, the law of attraction is just one component in creating the joyful and abundant life you desire, the same way that flour is just one ingredient needed to make a pie; you can't make a pie without flour; without flour it tastes terrible!

When I learned the Universal laws that I'm sharing with you, and began applying them to my life, I realized that there is so much more to co-creating an extraordinary life than simply visualizing what you want and expecting it to appear. Once you learn each of these laws and understand how they fit together, things that you would have formerly described as miracles start to happen.

To create a piece of fabric, you must weave together what is called the "warp" yarns and the "weft" yarns. The warp consists of the yarns that run up and down vertically, and the weft refers to the yarns that run right to left. You first lay the warp down on the loom and then you begin weaving in the weft. The way I like to think about working with these Universal laws is that the weft represents the seven laws, and the warp represents the principle of trust. Each law has to be woven together with trust – trust in the laws themselves, and trust that you are deserving of receiving everything that you desire. This merging is what creates the fabric of a fabulous life. Trust helps us strengthen our minds; it improves our ability to direct our thoughts, and it deepens our connection with our innermost self.

Experimenting with these laws in your everyday life is a bit like making a commitment to going to the gym. You can't work out once and expect to suddenly be fit. Getting in shape is a process that involves going back every few days and slowly building your endurance and muscles. It's the same way with learning. You must practice what you have learned, both to improve and to allow the new concepts to become part of you, to become second nature in your life. As you continue to do the inner work that I'm presenting to you here, your mind, body, and spirit will meet you halfway. You will find yourself growing stronger and stronger. In the same way that your muscles begin to show definition as a result of lifting weights, the true essence of your soul starts to shine brighter in the world, and begins to spread to others. And the cool thing – which we touched on already in the chapter about the law of attraction – is that the light that you spread to others will come back to you. When we get out of our own way, we clear a space for our soul, our innermost self, to guide us toward the path that will lead us to our greatest fulfillment. This is the essence of the Law of Allowing.

Look anywhere in the natural world, and you'll see that creation happens effortlessly. Trees don't *try* to grow; they simply grow. Birds don't overthink their yearly migration, they simply move according to the natural impulses that arise from within. You are every bit as much a part of nature as any plant or animal, and when you apply the law of allowing, your true nature – that of harmony, love and perfect timing – begins to blossom in your life effortlessly.

There are two primary ways to understand and apply the law of allowing. The first is by learning to allow others to be as they are, and the second is by allowing ourselves to receive from the Universe all that we desire. Let's look at each of these aspects of allowing.

Each one of us is born a unique individual, here to pursue our own interests and to express our unique talents in the ways that bring us joy and fulfillment. The fact that we are all so different is a vital part of our life experience. Without variety, we could never clarify want we want for ourselves. If you can understand this, and come to accept and even embrace another person's differences, you will be practicing the law of allowing, and life will begin to occur more easily for you. But if you step out of alignment with the law of allowing, and start to believe that your happiness – or security, or peace of mind – is contingent on how another person thinks, feels, acts, or believes, life becomes a constant, uphill battle. Anytime we believe that our happiness is dependent upon another person, situation, or external condition, we inevitably try to control that condition. This not only causes great suffering in our relationships, but it is also the source of untold and unnecessary stress.

We are all born with free reign over our own thoughts, emotions, beliefs, words and actions – but if you try to exert this control over another, you will never experience freedom. Trying to control another is the very definition of bondage, because it's an unwinnable pursuit. Contrary to what you may have been taught by well-meaning parents, lovers, or teachers, others are not here to "make us happy." One of our most primary missions in life is to learn how to access happiness within ourselves – regardless of what those around us do or don't do.

The opposite of allowing is resisting. When you are in a state of resistance – whether you are resisting another person's behavior, or some personality trait within yourself – you block the law of allowing from bringing ease into your life. It's as if the Universe is raining blessings down upon you, but in your resistance, you have an umbrella up that keeps it from coming in. There is great freedom and ease in allowing circumstances to be what they are and in allowing people to be who they are, whether you agree with them or not. Practicing the Law of Allowing means granting others the same rights you ask for yourself – the rights to be, do, and have whatever you choose, without someone else trying to stop you due to their own emotional attachments.

We give ourselves a great gift when we allow others to be who they are and to honor their right to live their lives as they choose. They are neither right nor wrong. They simply "are" who they are.

The second application of the law of allowing is in relation to how open we are to receiving the things we desire. All human beings vacillate between being in a state of receptivity and being in a state of resistance, and there are many shades of grey between those two extremes. So how can you tell in any moment if you are open to receiving the things you desire? It's easy. Just by paying attention to your emotions. In general, the better you feel, the more you are allowing.

Good-feeling emotions such as ease, relief, comfort, and peace are indications that you are open to allowing the things you have asked for to flow into your experience. If you think about this logically, it makes sense: when you are relaxed and at ease, you are more perceptive of what is going on around you. You hear more clearly what people are saying, you see possibilities and opportunities that present themselves, and you have the mental bandwidth to make correlations that you miss completely when you are feeling stress.

The exact opposite is true when we are in a state of resistance. When the fight-or-flight nervous system is engaged – meaning we are experiencing some degree of fear, angst, anger, or tension of any kind – all of our resources are channeled into surviving whatever situation we encounter as the source of our stress. In this state, it's impossible to be receptive. In fact, we shut ourselves down – emotionally, mentally, and physically – in an attempt to distance ourselves from uncomfortable feelings. As a result, we lose access to the broader, wiser aspects of ourselves, and we often can't see solutions that are right in front of us.

It's so easy to blame other people or situations for not giving us what we want or need, but by understanding the Law of Allowing, we begin to realize that the life we desire is available to us at every moment; it's only our resistance that keeps it from us. When we release the resistance, we become receptive again, and walk the path to all the success and joy we desire.

Putting the Law of Allowing Into Action:

Simply put, applying the Law of Allowing is "getting out of your own way," and it is easier than you might think. It is about making a deliberate decision to notice and then move away from your patterns of resistance. Trying to change something or someone outside your sphere of influence will *always* create resistance within you, so anytime you notice yourself doing this, you can remind yourself that the only power you have in any moment is the power to change the way *you* think and feel.

Along with releasing any attempt to control the people and things around you, practice also releasing your attachment to how others view you. None of us really knows what another is experiencing, and we waste a lot of precious energy trying to figure that out – and even more energy trying to modify our behavior in order to please them. The more you relinquish the illusion of control, the more receptive you will be, and the abundance of the Universe will rush in to fill that space.

CHAPTER 4:

The Law of Sufficiency & Abundance

The next beautiful Gift is the law of sufficiency and abundance. It's important to understand this universal law because we live in a world where – spiritually, energetically, and physically – there is an unlimited supply of resources for each of us to create the experiences that we most want. Look anywhere in the nature and you will notice that there is abundance in all things: an abundance of air to breathe; an abundance of water that flows, an abundance of seeds that continue to regenerate into the food that sustains us, an abundance of ideas that cause art and science and technology to continue evolving and thriving...

Most people confuse the Universal energy of abundance with the physical condition of having money in the bank. But our world is full of abundance that is simply part of our human experience. The very fact that the sun rises every morning and that our earth continues to revolve in perfect balance with all other planets is evidence of the natural abundance of this life.

Manifestations of the abundance we want to create in our life is ours for the taking; it is part of our divine inheritance. There is no end to this supply. It is constantly regenerating and finding new avenues to flood into our life experience – IF we are open to receive them.

Most of us have been trained not to see the world through the eyes of abundance, but instead through eyes of limitation. We take for granted the natural wonders like those I just described, and focus instead on what we don't have. We become obsessed with amassing more and more things. The grand irony of our pursuit of material abundance is that the only reason we desire more of anything is because we believe we will feel better – more at ease or happier – when we get them. We miss the fact that the real purpose behind our search for money or success is to feel good. We miss the fact that feeling good is something we can accomplish right now and in every moment.

Just consider this for a moment: is there any restriction to the amount of laughter you can experience? Is there any limit to how much love you can feel? The answer is of course not. Such experiences, and countless others are yours for the having in as much abundance as you desire to have them. Abundance is flowing all around us. We are the ones who hold ourselves back from experiencing it.

Some pretty incredible things begin to happen when you believe in your own abundance and let it take root and grow inside you. Speaking from my own experience, I realized first that there are always many more paths to the things we desire than we usually give ourselves permission to see. Second, I learned that shifting the way we look at the world from a lens of lack, to a lens of abundance, is what opens up the floodgates.

When I was in college, working toward my degree in Architectural Design, there was a definite point at which I felt that I would never succeed. This was in an era before computers had the ability to do all that they can today. Now, with the press of a button, a computer can generate on screen the dimensions of a living space and then add images of each potential piece of furniture in order to get a feel for the room's design. Within moments the designer can create a visual of his or her design in such a way as to clearly communicate it to a client. But back then, we had a drafting table, and used a T-square and a triangle to draw every element by hand: first by drawing a grid and then by building up to create the perspective of the room. Not only was this time-consuming; it frustrated me. I didn't want to become a designer so that I could spend all my time calculating and drawing dimensions; I wanted to spend my time creating beautiful spaces.

At the end of my first year, I told my rendering teacher about the difficulties I was having, and that I was seriously considering changing majors. He suggested that I buy a sketchbook and draw ten drawings a day over the summer. Then he explained that I was to sketch each one without looking at my paper. He said this would develop my eye/hand coordination so that in time I would be able to stare at the shape and size of an object while drawing it accurately onto paper.

I did as my professor suggested and faithfully went about drawing ten different things a day. Each time I finished, I was so disappointed in what I had drawn: the lines were overlapping; the objects were misshapen, and nothing looked real, but I kept at it. At the end of summer I looked through the whole notebook and was so upset that it wasn't filled with beautiful drawings that I threw the whole sketchbook in the garbage. I felt like a failure, and that my dream job would forever be out of reach – but, as it so often does, the Universe had other plans.

I went back to college and the first project we were given included making seven different renderings. I will never forget feeling something "click" inside me, like a snap of a finger, and suddenly I could draw freehand. Now I had a much faster and more fluid way of transferring my ideas and thoughts to the page. I still had to use a grid to create scale, but I could freehand the furnishings, the windows, door, fabrics, lighting, and all the interiors in the room. My delight grew when the next day we were given watercolors and watercolor paper to play with. I loved everything about it and discovered then that I was a natural painter.

I had tapped into an abundance of talent within me that I never knew existed – and an abundance of new ideas for how to execute those talents. I began doing all my renderings on watercolor paper, and then bringing them to life with watercolors. My style had evolved naturally and was distinct and unique. I had no idea that a few short years later I would use my talent to create fine art and had already established my own signature style.

Everything we need to create the magnificent life experience we desire is within our reach – not just enough to get by, but in abundance. This includes the talents and abilities that are still waiting to be tapped within you, and it includes every possible path to your realization of them. Looking through the eyes of lack and limitation had me believe that the only way to the final outcome I wanted was to surrender to an outdated and laborious method of doing things. When I finally opened up to the possibility that there might be another way, I was not only led around the limitation; I was delivered into, what ultimately became for me, a very successful career as an architectural designer and then as an artist.

In every moment, and in every important aspect of life, there is an abundance of these types of clues available to us. We cannot find them – or more accurately, we cannot *feel* them – if we are convinced they're not there, or if we've resigned ourselves to the belief that life is a struggle. Beliefs based in limitation or lack drastically reduce the number of options we can perceive in any given moment, which then drastically affects the ease with which we are able to reach our goals and fulfill our desires.

Most of us have bought into the belief that who we are, what we have, and the talents we were born with are not enough. This is not only a lie; it's also a powerful self-fulfilling prophesy. You know from what you've already learned about the law of attraction that what we think and feel draws resonant experiences to us. If you feel that life is hard, that you are lacking in some way, or that nothing you do is ever good enough, that is the quality of the experiences that you will tend to attract into your life. If you feel you are not enough, you are right. If you feel what you have is not enough, you will continue to draw to you the experience of not having enough.

The truth is that right now, you have everything within you to make your life a living dream. In the same way that you were born entitled to the air you breathe and the sun that warms you and gives you light, you were born absolutely worthy of experiencing all the abundance you desire. You have everything you need inside of you to build a fortune and to reach your goals. You have all the talent you need to create your ideal career, and to attract your ideal mate.

The only thing standing between you and anything you right now desire is you. In every moment, you are the one who makes the choice to focus on the abundance that is all around you or to focus on lack. You are the one who has the power to implement these powerful Universal laws and principles into your life, or not. Living a more abundant life is not about time or about money. It requires only a change in perception and attitude.

Putting the Law of Sufficiency & Abundance into Action

To apply the law of sufficiency and abundance in your life, commit to becoming more mindful of and, eventually, the master of - your internal dialogue. When you find yourself looking at situations in your life and thinking, "All the good men/women have been taken," or "I don't have enough money," or "There is too much competition for the job I want," remember that this is the signal that you are sending out, and that the law of attraction is responding to, and in that moment, change it. The Universe is always listening.

CHAPTER 5:

The Law of Pure Potentiality

The fifth Universal gift that governs manifestation is the law of pure potentiality. This law acknowledges that there is an eternal, non-physical field of consciousness that underlies everything in our physical Universe. Pure potentiality, or pure consciousness, is the invisible source from which everything in the manifested world originates – including our self. When we realize that we are, at our core, part of this unlimited stream of pure consciousness or potentiality, we tap into the power to create anything we desire. In this dimension of time and space, there are literally an infinite number of ways that the energy of pure consciousness can manifest into tangible form, and each of us receives this energy in our own unique ways.

In my own life, my awareness of pure potentiality first emerged as a desire to paint. I remember the night I woke up in the middle of the night and felt overcome by the need to paint. I got out of bed, grabbed my paints, water, brushes and 2 large watercolor pieces of paper and sat on my kitchen floor and started painting. When I finished, I was staring at two faces, one on each paper – a creation had just poured through me and I knew I had tapped into a Universal stream of pure consciousness; the pure expression of my soul. Not long later I gave up designing and started painting full time.

At that point in my life, I had not yet learned to meditate, but I have always had a daily practice of prayer. Each time before I painted, I would pray to God to allow divine energy to flow from heaven through my arms and hands and onto the canvas or paper. I even began writing a prayer on the canvas or paper before beginning to paint. When this energy was flowing through me, I could easily sketch and paint a single painting in one sitting. When I was done, I'd step back in awe and unable to believe I had just painted that. I would thank God for allowing all that creative energy to flow through me. I was aligned with the creative power that creates everything in our Universe, and it was pouring out of me.

The impulse to paint in the middle of the night continued over a period of a few years; I'd wake up with images of people in my head, and would feel overwhelmed with a need to paint them and to bring them to life. I showed my art in many galleries and still sell at the Portland Art Museum Rental Sales Gallery, but I never chose to sell any of the faces I'd created in the middle of the night. Somehow I knew they were a gift from spirit. And although some were stolen when my farmhouse studio and gallery was robbed 16 years ago, years later a family member bought the stolen pieces at a garage sale in another city.

Incredibly, they found their way back to me, or at least to my extended family.

The experience of painting taught me that I have access to an energy within me that is divine and spirit-led. This energy continued to be available to me even after I stopped painting full time. It was my connection to this flow of pure consciousness and pure potentiality that, years later, led me to pursue the field of life coaching and hypnotherapy, and to share the success I found through these practices with others.

In the period of time following my daughter's brain injury, I stopped painting. Looking back, I can see that while this was in part out of necessity, it was also a reflection of how I had temporarily shut down my connection to the energy of pure potentiality. It is so easy to allow circumstances – particularly painful ones – to distract us from the flow of this energy in our lives. But it's important to realize that even if we are blocking it by giving greater attention to our fear or our anguish, the energy never stops flowing; it is still available to us at any given time. It took 6 years, but the creative energy to paint opened up again, and even though I am not spending time doing it now, I know I will again when I have the time.

The fears and uncertainties that we impose on ourselves are the only true limitations we face. When we seek security or validation in the people or circumstances around us, we live in fear of what might happen, and of how people will react. Our orientation to life becomes what Deepak Chopra has termed "object-referral": rather than focusing our attention fully on our own inner being and on the energy of pure potentiality-flowing through us, we become fixated on external circumstances and therefore are unable to receive that flow.

The solution is to become what Chopra calls "self-referred," a state in which we are connected to, and intimate with, our own inner world. It is a state in which we know our inner being, our soul, as the source of all that manifests in our lives. In this state of receptivity, the energy of pure potentiality flows freely to us and through us in an infinite number of ways.

Putting the Law of Pure Potentiality into Action:

We have already explored how the practices of meditation and journaling are powerful ways to connect with the field of consciousness that is the source of all things, and these practices are extremely effective ways to increase your awareness of the energy of pure potentiality. When you allow yourself to be silent and just "be," you develop a connection with this underlying field, with your soul, and begin to see the ways in which it expresses itself all around you.

Another powerful way to connect with the field of pure potentiality is to notice and actively appreciate its many expressions in the physical Universe. Regularly spending time in nature is a great way to become aware of the intelligence within every living thing. When you see a beautiful sunset, or listen to the waves of the ocean crash up against the shore, or smell the beautiful scent of a flower, remind yourself that these are all physical manifestations of pure potentiality, and that you have access to this same energy stream.

When you come to rest in the truth of who you are – an extension of the energy that creates all things – you will begin to realize that there are no limits to how much of this life-force you can allow to flow through you, and no boundaries to all that you can create.

CHAPTER 6:

The Law of Detachment

The sixth Universal Gift is the law of detachment. This principle states that in order to acquire anything in the physical Universe, we must relinquish our attachment to it. It's important to understand that relinquishing our attachment to something is not the same as relinquishing our desire for it. Rather, it's letting go of the illusion that we have any measure of control over how or when or through what avenues our desired outcomes will unfold.

Detachment requires a loosening of our ego's idea that there are very specific conditions that need to be in place in order for us to be happy. It is the realization that we simply do not have a broad enough perspective to be able to see all the possibilities available to us, or to recognize all the opportunities for growth that often appear right in front of us. Detachment requires us to acknowledge that sometimes the path to our greatest fulfillment comes disguised as loss or tragedy.

Life taught me the most about the law of detachment seven plus years ago, when my eldest daughter, who had just begun her career as a surgical nurse, was in a horrific accident that left her with a traumatic brain injury. Simultaneously, I discovered that my husband of 25 years was having an affair with a young girl who was the same age as our eldest daughter. Hearing this, our youngest daughter dropped off the map; she simply couldn't process all the upheaval.

I did not realize it at the time, but this dramatic coming apart of the life I had known was actually preparing me for the next step in my spiritual awakening. It was during this period, as I searched deeply for answers, that I discovered the Quantum Success Coaching Academy and was introduced to all the concepts I am sharing with you here. In the process of letting go, I was finally open to receive the clues that had been all around me.

The law of detachment helped me to accept where I was, where my girls were, and to begin to view all that had happened from a broader perspective. Before I understood this, I had felt gripped by the feeling that I was a victim, and it was my attachment to this perspective that was blocking me from healing. The law of detachment taught me that every life experience comes bearing gifts, and if we are open to it, life will deliver us something far more than we could ever dream for ourselves.

Prior to the upheaval following the discovery of my husband's affair, my happiness and sense of security had been centered around making sure my life looked the way I thought it was supposed to: creating the "perfect" family, making the "perfect" home, and hosting the "perfect" dinner parties. As that illusion of perfection fell away, I began to define my life by an entirely different set of values. Getting to know myself more deeply and being strong for my girls became the compass by which I guided my life. I was stepping onto a new path in life, and even though I was terrified by the idea that I no longer knew who I was or where that path would lead me, at least I was feeling movement where there had so long been stagnation.

As I continued to apply these Universal laws of creation – and the law of detachment in particular – I began to heal, and my whole life started changing for the better. I discovered that the more I trusted, the easier it was to get out of my own way. I was truly allowing God, the Universe, and the broader, wiser aspect of myself to guide my heart and inform my choices.

I did the inner work on myself that I now teach others in my webinar "Creating the Life You Desire, "and new doors began to open. I met the most beautiful man, whom I have been with for over six years now. I found the perfect place to live downtown and was able to purchase it at an amazing price, weeks before the prices shot up. My younger daughter is starting to show up more, and even though my older daughter's healing was a process that took seven years, she is now married to a wonderful young man and they just had a beautiful baby girl.

These things did not "just happen." They unfolded in perfect timing as I continued to apply these Universal laws. I was able to move through life with a newfound patience and trust. When we align with the law of detachment, we no longer feel the need to force life to occur. We relax, trust, and allow life to unfold itself in its own wise way.

Putting the Law of Detachment into Action:

One of the most powerful ways to access the law of detachment is through the practices of meditation and journaling. When you meditate, you connect to your soul, your innermost self; the part of you that can intuitively knows what is in your highest good. And when you follow your meditation period with a few minutes of journaling, you'll find that as you write you are either releasing emotions that you're holding onto that no longer serve you, or you are tapping into new ideas that lead you to your true path in life.

When you reconnect with the larger part of you that knows your heart's desires, you naturally begin to release everything that stands in the way of its continued expression. As you allow this expression to flow, you will find yourself inspired with new ideas and new actions. For myself, and my clients, the period following daily meditation often proves to be the most creative and productive of the day. Any process that allows you to quiet your mind and to rest in the space between thoughts is an effective tool for entering a meditative state, and will help you get more deeply in touch with your soul self.

As you continue to practice the law of detachment, you will find yourself more and more drawn to your inner world – to the changing landscape of your thoughts, moods, impulses and emotions. The more time and attention you give to this innermost aspect of you, the more you will begin to see the external changes you desire. As synchronicities begin to appear all around you, you will know you are on the right path, and you'll begin feeling the joy and happiness life has to offer.

CHAPTER 7:

The Law of Polarity

The seventh and final Universal law is the law of polarity, which is simply recognition that there are two poles, or opposites, in everything that exists. For example, on the subject of temperature, on one end of the extreme is the experience of "hot," and at the other is the experience of "cold." While both extremes can be objectively measured in degrees, every individual has his or her own subjective experience of what the spectrum of hot is, and what is cold.

In the same way that hot and cold mean different things to different people, so do extremes like rich and poor, love and hate, good and bad, etc. There is no one Universal definition for any experience; everything is relative, and the only reason we are able to experience anything at all is because of the law of polarity.

For example, if the things you perceive as "bad" did not exist, would you be able to recognize what you consider to be a "good" experience? If hunger was not part of your experience, could you ever appreciate the sensation of being satisfied? If failure did not exist, would you know what it feels like to experience success? The answer to these questions is no, because we live in a universe of contrasting values, and it takes one extreme to know the other.

The law of polarity teaches us that this experience we call human life exists along a broad spectrum of possibilities ranging from what each of us considers outrageously positive to tragically negative – and an infinite number of points in between. It teaches us that there would be no way to realize something we want unless we are also aware of what we do not want. In the presence of one, we are more powerfully aware of the other. Within each experience, regardless of whether you view it as positive or negative, exists the potential to experience its polar opposite: it is in the moments when you feel tired and run down that you're the most aware of wanting to feel vital and alive. When you realize you don't have enough money, you become acutely aware that you want an abundance of it. If you're in the middle of a difficult or unfulfilling relationship, you know for certain that you want greater harmony.

Once we find this clarity, we have a powerful decision to make: we can continue to focus on the contrast, or we can choose to focus on the clarity. Which one you choose will have a dramatic influence on the outcome you achieve. Remember that everything that manifests into our lives – whether we regard it as good, bad, or with indifference – is drawn to us through the powerful law of attraction. Where our attention goes, energy flows, and this energy is returned to us though the moment-to-moment unfolding of our life experiences. The key to manifesting the experiences that you desire is to give as much of your attention as you possibly can in every moment to that which you want, rather than on that which you don't want.

Putting the Law of Polarity into Action:

To use the Law of Polarity to your advantage, you first have to make peace with it. Contrasting experiences are a necessary part of life. In the same way we could never enjoy the experience of being warm if we had never been cold, or of satisfaction if we had never experienced hunger, contrast helps us profoundly to discover what we want. It is the fuel that powers our evolution; that inspires us to continually reach for more.

When contrast shows up in your life – whether in big ways or small – acknowledge briefly what it is you don't want (for example, "I don't want to be in debt," or "I don't want to be a cigarette smoker."). Once the contrast has provided you with this valuable clarity, it is then important to take your focus off of what you don't want as quickly as possible, and to redirect it onto what you do want instead. In my webinar "Creating the Life you Desire," I guide participants through a powerful exercise that helps them transform painful contrast into exhilarating clarity. They then use this clarity as a starting point for summoning the energy of whatever they now desire to create.

Remember that everything that manifests in the external world of form and phenomenon is created first in the inner world of desires, prayers, ideas, thoughts, feelings, and energy.

The faster you can bring your vibration into harmony with your desire *having already been fulfilled,* the more effortlessly you will magnetize the resources to accomplish exactly that. The inner and outer parts of ourselves work in this same way. If we do our inner work first through meditating, journaling, and working with a counselor or life coach, then when we are ready to take action, the doors fly wide open and we are suddenly on our true path in life; the path that brings us the greatest joy.

For example, if you desire to lose twenty pounds, use the full power of your mind and imagination to conjure what it would feel like to be twenty pounds lighter. How would it feel physically, and even more important, how does it feel emotionally? Do you feel proud? Confident? Beautiful? Free? The weight loss you desire will naturally take some time to occur, but you can achieve the feeling state of having already accomplished it right now, and that emotional state helps you stay focused and do the things it takes to lose that 20 pounds.

The Law of Polarity speeds the rate at which all things we desire can make their way into our lives; but it requires a shift in mindset for most people. Rather than applying external actions to try to "make" ourselves beautiful or feel more confident, we can tap directly into the power of bathing ourselves in feeling beautiful, confident; and this energy will attract to us the outcomes we desire – from the inside out.

CHAPTER 8:

Putting It All Together

The Universal gifts that I've shared with you throughout these pages have always been with me, interwoven throughout my life, and I have used them to bring about many positive outcomes, although at times I was unaware of what I was doing. The exciting thing is that as you become aware of these gifts, you begin to consciously co-create along with this beautiful energy available to all of us.

One of the nicest ways to start experiencing this is by using the tools I teach in my online master class called "Creating The Life You Desire." In fact, this course is designed after the process that I used in my own life, which brought about dramatic results very quickly.

When I was going through my divorce, it had been a little over a year and I finally felt ready to move on in life. I created what is called a Desire Statement. I did this to get clear of the type of man I wanted to attract in to my life. I started the process of getting clear about what I wanted in a relationship this time around. I began by writing down all the things I experienced in my old relationship that I knew I didn't want in my life ever again. As I read through each item, I took the time to get very clear about what I now wanted in a relationship.

When I was 20, which is the age I was when I met my ex-husband, and my thoughts about the man I wanted in my life were: cowboy, who skied, cute, blond hair, etc. Now 30 years later my words were: integrity, trustworthy, honest, kind, loves me the same way I love him, loves my kids, I can talk to him about anything and visa-versa, brings joy and laughter into each day, and likes to be healthy and active, wants to travel and see the world and is mature enough to talk things through in a nice way. As I was writing all these qualities down, I was using the Law of Deliberate Creation to actively send out into the Universe the type of man I wanted to spend the rest of my life with.

After I teach clients how to make their desire statement, I have them say it out loud with gusto, once or twice a day, every day until things start showing up for them. I began doing that myself, hence I realize now that I was using the law of attraction to draw to me what I really wanted in a relationship. Every time I became discouraged thinking nothing was happening, I was able to rise above this "victim mentality," and now with the awareness of my negative feelings, I was able to reject them and replace them with what I really wanted. I began to get out of my own way and learned to trust on a higher level then I ever had in my life, and in so doing, was utilizing the law of Allowing. (The law of Allowing)

I decided to go on Match.com and almost immediately I had a very nice looking man ask me to send him a few photos, so I did, with in minutes he sent me an email with about 10 photos, and when I got to jpeg #7 there he stood almost naked in front of a mirror. I was new at this dating thing and was just shocked, I wrote back to him and told him I really liked his profile and all his pictures, until I got to jpeg #7. Politely, I told him thanks, but no thanks, and feeling very discouraged, I took myself off Match. I had not dated for or 30 years and was not ready for this new way of dating at all.

I pouted for a few days, then again, realizing I was falling into that "poor me; victim" feeling, I decided I would not let this get me down. I asked for divine timing to come into the equation, and to give me peace about how everything would unfold. I didn't need to know when, but, embracing the Law of Detachment, I began stepping back into saying my desire statement faithfully. I meditated each day and visualized myself with a walking with a man, hand in hand, with a comfortable and peaceful feeling. I didn't know it but I was doing my inner work, and taking action by saying my desire statement each day (Law of Polarity).

I began to feel comfortable in my own skin, and, even though I was going through a really hard time with my daughters, I felt peaceful and happy inside. I knew innately that my life was on a new path, and that felt peaceful. I felt like my true path in life was unfolding, but I trusted he would. (Law of Pure Potentiality)

About three weeks later a friend invited me to a party downtown. I told her yes, but the day of the party I was helping my daughter on her little farm, cleaning out the chicken coop and bunny cage in the pouring rain, which left me freezing cold, dirty and wet. I was on the ferry on the way back to my house and it was raining sideways when my friend called and asked when I'd be there. The guests were all downtown having happy hour together. I lived about 35 minutes from Portland at the time. I told my friend I wasn't going to make it. It was so rainy, I was hungry and planned to go home, take a shower, have a bite to eat and go straight to bed. She begged me to call her after I'd eaten and taken my shower, so I agreed. When I called I was feeling much better and decided to head down, even though I'd be an hour plus late. She mentioned quickly that, "Oh I forgot; it's a dress up 70's party!" They even had a one-hit wonder band playing.

I had nothing to wear. Then I thought about an outfit I still had from my 30th birthday. It was a 70's mini dress, but in a classy way. I had a long silk scarf which I tied backwards on my neck, put some boots on, walked out my garage door, got in my car and left. About halfway down the mountain I realized it was raining so hard and I left so quickly, I didn't put a coat on or even have an umbrella! Well, my positive attitude and I decided, *I'll find a place in front, it will be ok...*but it wasn't. There was nowhere to park for blocks. Really bummed out, I turned up the street and was heading home.

In front of me I saw a restaurant owned by a friend I'd grown up with, and in front was a kid standing in the pouring rain, valet parking. Suddenly, I got an idea. I pulled up and I asked if he was busy tonight and he said, "No it's so stormy, we're really slow." I said, "Would you ever hop in and let me drive you down about 7 blocks, hop out at this party, then you can valet my car and Ill come get it later?" Looking back, I know this was an outrageous question, but for some reason I thought it was a great solution. He said "oh no, this is my first day, I'd get fired." I said, "No, you can blame it on me. Bruce and I have been friends since first grade." Excited, the valet told me Bruce was his uncle. "No way," I said. "Who's your mom?" It turns out; I knew her mom and had just talked to her on Facebook about a week prior. Based on this, the boy decided my crazy offer was OK. He hopped in my car, and dropped me off at the front door of the restaurant.

When I think about the unfolding of these events all these years later, I can't believe I ever ended up at this party. My old self would have stayed home, curled up in bed and watched a movie.

Little did I know that the love of my life would be in this room. The moment I walked in, my girlfriend grabbed me and immediately two boys showed up introducing themselves. One of them is the gentleman I am with now.

We began dating and taking things slowly, and about three months later, I pulled out my desire statement. Sure enough, he was every single thing I had asked for. He is the best partner and I am so grateful that I was mindful of my inner dialogue that night and allowed myself to follow my intuition (law of sufficiency and abundance) and ended up at that party. If I hadn't, the Universe would have had to find another way for us to meet!

CONCLUSION:

A Framework for All Creation

"Truth is by nature self-evident. As soon as you remove the cobwebs of ignorance that surround it, it shines clear."
- Mahatma Gandhi

The ignorance that Gandhi speaks of is still rampant in our world, for the simple reason that most of us learned to approach life in one of two primary ways: by unconsciously falling in line with the attitudes, strategies, and belief systems that were modeled by our caregivers and teachers; or by rebelling against them, and trying desperately to do the opposite. In either case, it is rare that any one of us is given any information at all about the forces that organize and sustain our life experience, let alone any guidance about how to maximize that experience. As a result, we become a little wiser as we make our way through the proverbial school of hard knocks, but often without a framework to understand why we attract the experiences we do or what we can do to change them when they fail to satisfy us.

Through trial and error, we manage to find success in some aspects of life even as we fall short in others. Without an understanding of the power of consciously aligning ourselves with the forces that are at work behind the scenes, we come to rely on words and actions alone, mistakenly believing that as human beings, these are our most powerful tools for creating. As we have learned, they are not.

No one can argue that some things can be accomplished through action alone. You can accomplish something through action... but it does take your brain to set your body in motion. Any able-bodied person can move a pile of rocks from one place to another, and by applying the same principles of hard work and persistence we can create a certain amount of success. But words and actions alone are not sufficient to fulfill our true goals in life – to experience peace, happiness, joy, love, abundance, and connection. These experiences unfold only when we open up and share the truest parts of ourselves and develop an unwavering connection to the energy of this beautiful Universe, the Universe God created for all of us. When we make this connection, we create on an entirely different scale, and the effects ripple into every part of our lives.

Begin to pay closer attention, and you will find evidence of these Universal laws silently at work all around you. They are free, abundant, and ours for the taking – but we have to be aware of them in order to make use of the incredible gifts they offer. As you put into action the principles shared throughout this book, evidence of their truth will appear in your life and you will begin to see their power for yourself. The cobwebs that Gandhi refers to – of outworn strategies and limiting beliefs – will fall away; and like the sun reemerging after a good rain, bringing out a deeper hue and newness in everything below, you too will come to understand the power and radiance within you. Awareness is the key to begin opening up to these gifts, to basking in this beautiful energy that is everyone's birthright.

ABOUT THE AUTHOR

Jeanne Provost is the founder of Living Well Life Coaching and author of *Plugging In, Connecting To Your Universal Gifts*. Jeanne is a Life Coach and Hypnotherapist. You can join her coaching groups, receive private coaching, or attend her online classes, retreats, or meditation group. To learn more about Jeanne's work (and any upcoming events) join her e-mail list at www.livingwelllifecoaching.com.

Follow Jeanne

Facebook: https://www.facebook.com/LivingWellLifeCoaching/

Facebook: https://www.facebook.com/jeanneprovostauthor/

Linked In: https://www.linkedin.com/in/jeanne-provost-a120a052/

Instagram: https://www.instagram.com/livingwelllifecoaching/?hl=en

Twitter: https://twitter.com/jeanneMprovost

Made in the USA
Lexington, KY
07 September 2019